USA

SALLY GARRINGTON

Evans

TITLES IN THE COUNTRIES OF THE WORLD SERIES:

ARGENTINA • AUSTRALIA • BRAZIL • CANADA • CHINA
EGYPT • FRANCE • GERMANY • INDIA • ITALY • JAPAN
KENYA • MEXICO • NIGERIA • POLAND • UNITED KINGDOM
USA • VIETNAM

Published by Evans Brothers Limited
2A Portman Mansions
Chiltern Street
London W1U 6NR

Reprinted with revisions 2007

VISIT OUR WEBSITE
www.evansbooks.co.uk
Evans

Produced for Evans Brothers Limited by
Monkey Puzzle Media Ltd
Gissing's Farm, Fressingfield
Suffolk IP21 5SH
First published 2002
© copyright Evans Brothers Limited 2002

British Library Cataloguing in Publication Data
USA. - (Countries of the world)
1.United States - Juvenile literature
I.Title
973

ISBN 0 237 52806 1
13 - digit ISBN 978 0 237 52806 5

Editor: Polly Goodman
Designer: Jane Hawkins
Picture researcher: Lynda Lines
Map artwork by Peter Bull
Charts and graph artwork by Encompass Graphics Ltd

Endpapers (front): Rock formations in Monument Valley, on the Arizona/Utah border.
Title page: High-rise hotels on Miami Beach, Florida.
Imprint and Contents page: Mountains, lakes and forests in the Grand Teton National Park, Wyoming.
Endpapers (back): A marina in Honolulu, the capital city and main port of Hawaii.

Photographs were kindly supplied by the following: *Axiom* 9 Jenny Acheson, 46 Jenny Acheson; *Corbis* 10b James A. Sugar,
12 John McAnulty, 19 Reuters NewMedia Inc., 20 Neil Rabinowitz, 22 Jonathan Blair, 24 Doug Wilson, 27 Kelly-Mooney, 29
Charles O'Rear, 30t Nathan Benn, 30–31b Joseph Sohm, 32–33 Ed Kashi, 34 Raymond Gehman, 35 William A. Bake, 36 Anna
Clopet, 40 Yann Arthus-Bertrand, 42–43 Richard Cummins, 47 Gunter Marx, 50 Dave G. Houser, 53 Paul A. Souders, 54–55t
Joseph Sohm, 55b Jim Winkley/Eye Ubiquitous, 56 Reuters NewMedia Inc., 57 David Turnley; *Corbis Digital Stock* Front Cover
top, Front Cover bottom, 2–3, 17 (inset), 61 Bud Freund; *Courtesy of Central Artery Tunnel Project Public Information Dept* 41;
James Davis 42, 48; *Digital Vision* Title page, Imprint & Contents page, 10t, 23, 32 (inset), 37, 52, 60, 62–3; *Eye Ubiquitous* 13
Tim Page, 14 L. Fordyce; *Image Bank* Front Cover upper middle Harald Sund, 28 Harald Sund; *MPM Images* 38 Daniel Rogers;
NASA 18; *Photri* Front Cover lower middle, 8 Jeff Greenberg, 15, 16-17, 21, 44 Dennis MacDonald, 51 Jeff Greenberg; *Rex
Features* 26 Sipa Press, 43r Stuart Clarke, 49 Patrick Frilet/Sipa Press; *Robert Harding* 25, *Topham* 39 ImageWorks.

The US flag consists of 13 horizontal stripes representing the original 13 colonies, and 50 stars representing the 50 states that now make up the USA.

A view over the Grand Canyon National Park, in Arizona.

The USA is the wealthiest and most powerful country in the world. Much of its wealth is due to its size, and the diversity of its landscapes and people. It has only been independent since 1776, yet it has become the most influential country in the world. People from many lands have migrated to the USA to begin a new life, joining the Native Americans who have lived on the American continent for thousands of years.

The USA consists of 50 states, 48 of which adjoin each other. Two states are separate from the rest. Alaska lies to the west of Canada and is the largest of the US states. Hawaii is a group of volcanic islands in the Pacific Ocean.

A COUNTRY OF CONTRASTS

The USA is so big that there is a variety of climates, from the sub-tropical regions of Florida to the cooler, northern climates around New England. Its size also has an effect on local time. Across the 48 states there are four time zones, which means that when it is midnight in California, it is already 3 a.m.

KEY DATA

Area:	9,629,091km²
Highest Point:	Mt McKinley, Alaska (6,194m)
Lowest Point:	Death Valley, California (−86m)
Population:	297,000,000 (2004 estimate)
Birth rate per 1,000:	14.1 (2004)
Death rate per 1,000:	8.3 (2004)
GDP per Capita:	US$37,800* (2003)
Currency:	US Dollar ($)
Capital City:	Washington, District of Columbia
Major Cities:	New York (pop. 8,084,316) Los Angeles (pop. 3,798,981) Chicago (pop. 2,886,251)
Number of States:	50

* Estimate, calculated on Purchasing Power Parity basis
Sources: *CIA World Factbook, 2004*, US Census and American Factfinder

in New York. In Alaska, which is in a time zone behind California, it would be 11p.m. the previous evening.

Most Americans live in urban areas, but there are huge open landscapes that are used for recreation, and to escape the pressures of urban living. Some of these landscapes, such as the Grand Canyon, are among the most spectacular in the world.

Americans have the highest standard of living in the world. As a nation, Americans consume 25 per cent of the world's energy, yet the country only has about 5 per cent of the world's population.

American influence has travelled to most parts of the world, often through successful films and television shows. American food chains can now be found in towns and cities in all corners of the globe.

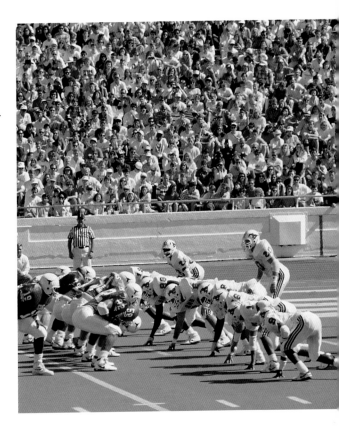

RIGHT: American football is an exciting team sport, played mainly in the USA and Canada.

The rocky cliffs of Big Sur, California, on the USA's west coast.

Mainland USA (not including Alaska) can be divided into three main regions: a mountainous area in the west, highlands in the east and a huge region of plains in the middle. In the west, the Rocky Mountains include several peaks over 4,270m high. The Great Plains of the interior are mostly below 400m. In the east are the Appalachian Mountains, which include the Blue Ridge Mountains. A coastal plain runs down the east of the USA and around the Gulf of Mexico, including the delta of the Mississippi River. Most of the eastern and southern coastline is low-lying, with many barrier islands and spits.

CASE STUDY
MOUNT ST HELENS ERUPTION

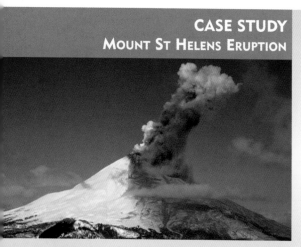

A cloud of ash rises from the top of Mount St Helens on 18 May, 1980.

Mount St Helens is a volcano in the Cascade Mountains. Here, the Juan de Fuca Plate is drawn beneath the North American Plate. In April 1980, a bulge appeared on the northern side of the volcano. On 18 May, an earthquake measuring 5.0 on the Richter scale caused a landslide. A massive explosion of gas and steam was followed by a towering ash cloud a few seconds later. An area of more than 500km^2 was devastated, with forests flattened by the blast and areas covered in a thick layer of ash. Although a devastating blow to the immediate plant and animal life, the volcano's eruption has brought new sources of nutrients to the surface which, over time, will benefit the soils of the region.

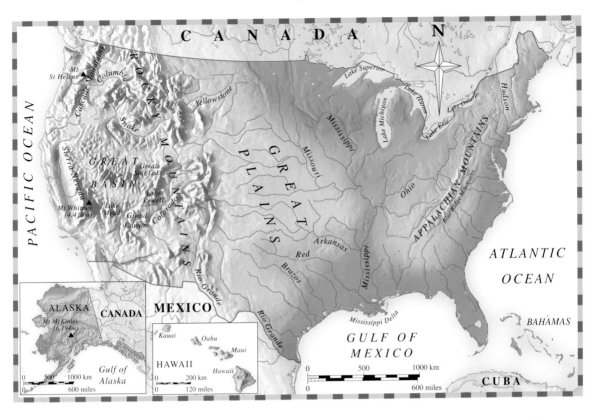

Rocky shores lie along the west coast and the coast of Alaska. The resistant rocks of these coasts form features such as headlands, arches and stacks. The land is constantly being changed by the forces of wind and water. Below the earth's surface there are other forces at work. Along the western side of the USA, there are several plate boundaries. These mark the edges of the large plates that make up the surface of the earth. Extreme heat within the earth sets up huge convection currents, which move the plates towards, away and past each other depending on the direction of flow.

CASE STUDY
THE NORTHRIDGE EARTHQUAKE

In California, the North American Plate and the Pacific Plate move next to each other within the San Andreas Fault System. Along certain sections, these plates lock together due to friction. Pressure builds up until one plate suddenly moves forward, causing an earthquake.

On 17 January 1994, an earthquake measuring 6.7 on the Richter scale occurred under the heavily populated suburb of Northridge, in Los Angeles. Even though California has invested heavily in earthquake-resistant buildings, there was a great deal of damage and 57 deaths. The damage was greater than expected because the epicentre of the earthquake was directly beneath the suburb. Much of the building damage was to older structures, built without earthquake-resistant designs. A stretch of elevated highway collapsed when the reinforced concrete gave way. It was here that most of the deaths occurred. Now the authorities are trying to ensure that older buildings are upgraded with earthquake-resistant materials, and imposing stricter regulations governing highway construction to try to be better prepared for the next movement of the earth.

AMERICAN RIVERS AND THEIR LANDFORMS

The USA has several large river systems, including the Mississippi in the east, the Columbia in the north-west and the Colorado in the south-west. The sources of the rivers are usually in upland areas. The source of the Columbia River is in the ice fields of the Canadian Rockies, whereas the Arkansas River, a tributary of the Mississippi, begins near Leadville, Colorado, in the US Rocky Mountains.

Each river drains an area known as its drainage basin. The Mississippi's drainage basin covers 41 per cent of the USA's total land area. In some parts of the country, rivers do not flow all year round. Rivers such as the San Gabriel in California are reduced to a trickle or nothing at all for part of the year.

Rivers alter the landscape in two ways: by erosion and by deposition.

EROSION

Erosion is more important in the upper sections of a river. Here, vertical erosion cuts down into the river bed, forming a V-shaped valley with steep sides. During heavy rainfall, material is washed down from the valley sides and adds to the river's load. The rock-covered river bed makes the flow uneven or turbulent. The river winds its way around areas of highland, which form interlocking spurs.

Many of these landscapes can be seen in the Rocky Mountains. In the upper section of the Arkansas River, in Colorado, the river drops 3,000m in just 200km. Here there are waterfalls and rapids that are also typical of the upper reaches of a river.

Gorges can be formed when there is a change in sea or land level. The Grand Canyon was formed many millions of years ago, when movements lifted the Colorado Plateau. As the plateau rose, the Colorado River cut down through it, carving out the deep gorge of the Grand Canyon.

TRANSPORTATION

Rivers carry material in different ways. Larger material is dragged along the river bed. Finer material is carried in the water. The Colorado's name means 'red-coloured' because it has been coloured red by the sediment in the water. Rivers erode their banks and beds with the material they carry. The faster a river flows, the more material it carries and the quicker it erodes.

DEPOSITION

In the lower sections of a river, deposition is the main process. The slope is gentler and rivers tend to move across their flood plains in a series of bends, called meanders. Within the

---

Riding the rapids over Hosum Falls on the White Salmon River, in Washington, USA.

meanders, erosion takes place at the outer edges and the river widens by lateral (sideways) erosion. Deposition occurs on the inside of a bend where the flow of water is slower. The neck of a meander can sometimes become so narrow that eventually the river cuts across the neck rather than flow round the meander. The meander is then abandoned and forms an oxbow lake. There are many oxbow lakes on the Mississippi flood plain in Louisiana. Eagle Lake, on the Louisiana-Missouri border, was known as Eagle Bend until the river took a short cut across the neck of the meander and made it a lake.

Sometimes rivers overflow their banks and deposit material on the flood plain. The coarsest material is dropped first and forms a natural embankment, called a levee.

Estuaries, such as the Roanoke River estuary in North Carolina, form where a river meets the sea. As the speed of the river slows down, it drops some of the material it is carrying. If this material blocks the main channel, the river is forced to flow round it in a number of small distributaries. If the ocean currents are not strong enough to remove material faster than it is being deposited a

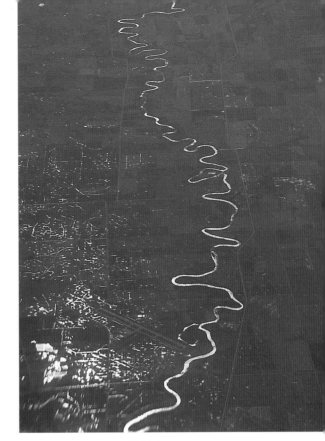

The Mississippi, the USA's longest river, meanders across its flood plain.

delta is formed. The Mississippi Delta, in Louisiana, formed where the Mississippi meets the Gulf of Mexico.

THE MISSISSIPPI COMPARED

River:	Mississippi	Nile	Amazon	Yangtze	Ganges
Continent:	North America	Africa	South America	Asia	Asia
Length, including tributaries (km):	6,019	6,484	6,516	5,800	2,700
Drainage area (km²):	4,160	2,881	7,180	1,970	1,073
Source:	N.W. Minnesota	Lake Tana	Andes	Tibetan Plateau	Himalayas

Source: *River Systems of the World* (www.rev.net)

The Mississippi Delta is steadily becoming more salty. This affects the region's farmlands.

MANAGEMENT OF THE MISSISSIPPI

The Mississippi is the largest river system in the USA, with 250 tributaries including the great Missouri River. It drains 31 states and carries 400 million tonnes of sediment down to the Gulf of Mexico each year. The river provides water for drinking and irrigation to towns along its banks and is the most important transport waterway in the USA.

The Mississippi's wide flood plain has been developed for agriculture and settlement. The river has been managed to improve flood control, water storage and navigation.

The Mississippi Delta is one of the largest in the world, but it is shrinking. Now that river management methods (see below) have partially controlled the flooding, less sediment

METHODS OF RIVER MANAGEMENT

Method	Action
Dams	Contain surplus flow to control flooding. Store water for irrigation and domestic use.
Concrete levees	Protect vulnerable towns from flooding. These replaced earth levees.
Removal of bankside vegetation	Makes water flow faster so the river is less likely to flood.
Control of dykes	Channels fastest flow into the centre of the river, so it is less likely to flood.
Removal of meanders	Reduces river's length and straightens channel, so it is less likely to flood. Helps navigation.
Spillways	Divert excess water away from major cities to a lake.

Source: US Corps of Engineers; American Rivers (www.americanrivers.org)

is being added to its flood plain and delta. At its mouth, waves in the Gulf of Mexico remove material from the delta, and salt water is now moving into the delta, destroying farmland.

Development along the river has caused several problems. Urban areas use the river to get rid of their domestic and industrial wastes and yet need the river as a water supply. Some stretches of the Mississippi are heavily polluted. Oil and gas extraction in the delta has also caused pollution. This has damaged some of the plants and animals that live there.

Farmers along the river have had to use chemical fertilisers to enrich their soils, because their land no longer receives sediment from the river floods. Excess nitrates from these fertilisers are washed into the river, causing algae and other plants to grow. The plants use up oxygen in the water, so there is not enough for animal life in the river. Farmers have also drained wetlands next to the river to increase their area of production. This means that when the river does flood, there is no natural use land to absorb the excess water.

CASE STUDY
THE MISSISSIPPI FLOODS OF 1993

In 1993, heavy rains fell in intense thunderstorms in the Midwest. An area the size of England was flooded at the point where the Ohio River meets the Mississippi, and more than 1,000 levees collapsed. Most of the government-built, concrete levees that protected the larger towns held firm, but 80 per cent of the earth levees failed. In total there were 50 deaths, and 75,000 people had to be evacuated from their homes. Huge areas of crops were destroyed. The floods caught people by surprise. The construction of the levees and other flood-control measures had made people feel safe, so large amounts of new housing and industry had been built on the flood plain. People felt so safe that many did not even have household insurance, and were left with nothing when their homes were destroyed in the floods.

In April 2001 another flood hit the Mississippi basin, the fourth serious flood since the disaster of 1993. Engineers have now realised that engineering methods alone

This road, in the state of Iowa, was closed by serious floods in 1993.

cannot prevent floods, and flood-control methods need to work with the river processes, not against them. Recently there have been moves towards putting back some of the river's meanders to slow its flow. In some areas, plans are in place to prevent further development on the flood plain. Farmers are being paid to allow some of their land to go back to being wetlands, so if the river overflows again, the wetland areas will act like sponges and absorb some of the excess water.

CLIMATES OF THE USA

The USA is so big that it has a wide range of climates, from sub-tropical in the south-east, to Arctic tundra in the north.

COASTAL CLIMATES

Climates near the coasts are the least extreme, because they are influenced by the oceans. In the south-east, around Florida, the climate is sub-tropical, with warm temperatures all year round and minimum monthly rainfalls of over 50mm. Vegetation is lush and palm trees thrive along the coasts. High humidity can make daily life uncomfortable, and there is a risk of hurricanes in the autumn, which often come ashore in this area.

In other warm southern and eastern coasts, the heat causes the build-up of cumulonimbus storm clouds, forming thunderstorms with heavy rain. All along the eastern coasts there is deciduous and coniferous woodland, depending on the soil type.

The west coast is drier in the south, with a more Mediterranean climate. California's warm dry summers continue to attract people to live there. The natural vegetation has adapted to the summer drought and is a mix of scrub oak and drought-resistant shrubs.

Further north on the west coast is the wettest region in the USA. Wet westerly winds from the Pacific Ocean are forced to rise over the mountains, and drop their moisture as rain on the western slopes. Here the area is heavily forested with conifers.

INTERIOR CONTINENTAL CLIMATE

The interior of the USA has a large temperature range, because the land heats and cools more rapidly further away from the oceans. There is little rainfall because the area is in the rain shadow of the Rockies. Prairie grasses that can cope with the cold winters and lack of rainfall are the natural vegetation. Tornadoes form over parts of this region because of the intense heat of the land.

DESERT CLIMATES

Desert climates are found in the south-west of the USA, in the rain shadow of the Rocky Mountains. Vegetation in this region has adapted to the climate. Cacti store water in their fleshy leaves, and other plants, such as blackbrush, have very small leaves to reduce water loss. Until very recently, these areas had low populations, but now cities such as Palm Springs and Las Vegas are attracting large numbers of people who enjoy the hot climate. Air-conditioning and the availability of water make a high standard of living possible.

MOUNTAIN CLIMATES

In the western mountains the climate changes with the altitude. Deciduous woodland grows lower down, with tundra and snowcaps in the peaks. Small populations have long made a living from the timber industry, but tourism is becoming increasingly important to these mountain areas. Towns such as Aspen are ski resorts in the winter and popular touring centres in the summer.

Waterfront houses in sub-tropical Miami.

16

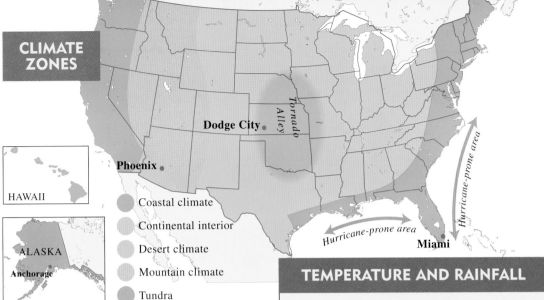

HAWAII

ALASKA

Anchorage

Dodge City

Tornado Alley

Phoenix

Hurricane-prone area

Hurricane-prone area

Miami

- Coastal climate
- Continental interior
- Desert climate
- Mountain climate
- Tundra

ARCTIC TUNDRA

Alaska has a tundra climate. The winters are very cold, but the southern coastal region can have mild summers because a warm current flows past this area. The southern region has dense conifer forests, although the growing season is only five months. Further north it is too cold for trees to grow and the vegetation is mostly lichens and mosses. The ground never thaws out completely, and this results in a permafrost layer. The larger centres of population in Alaska are in the warmer south.

The Grand Teton National Park, in north-west Wyoming, contains over 20 mountain peaks, each rising higher than 3,000m.

TEMPERATURE AND RAINFALL

Rainfall (mm) — DODGE CITY, KANSAS (778m) — Temp (°C)

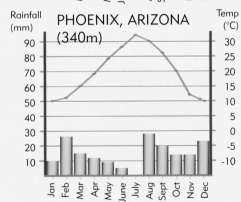

Rainfall (mm) — PHOENIX, ARIZONA (340m) — Temp (°C)

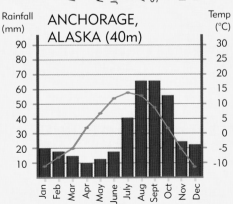

Rainfall (mm) — ANCHORAGE, ALASKA (40m) — Temp (°C)

KEY: Rainfall — Temperature

CLIMATIC HAZARDS

A climatic hazard is an extreme weather event that can threaten lives and property. The USA experiences a wide range of climatic hazards, including hurricanes, tornadoes, floods, droughts, blizzards and ice storms. They kill a number of people each year. The US government spends a lot of money on research into these hazards, to try to prevent their damage.

HURRICANES

Hurricanes are violent storms formed over warm oceans, around an area of very low pressure. As well as strong winds, they bring heavy rain, lightning and storm waves. The National Hurricane Center in Miami keeps a close watch on any tropical storms developing over the oceans, which might turn into hurricanes and move across the mainland. The Hurricane Center's predictions have become more accurate about the paths the hurricanes will take. Important information about weather systems is constantly being sent to the centre from weather satellites orbiting the earth.

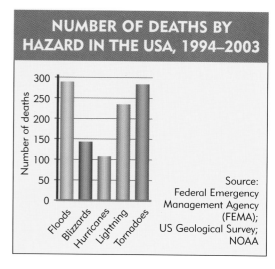

NUMBER OF DEATHS BY HAZARD IN THE USA, 1994–2003

Source: Federal Emergency Management Agency (FEMA); US Geological Survey; NOAA

A computer-generated image of Hurricane Fran, using information collected by a satellite. Hurricane Fran hit the USA's east coast in 1996.

BLIZZARDS AND THUNDERSTORMS

Blizzards can happen in many areas, but particularly in the eastern states. In January 2001 all three of New York City's airports were closed by blizzards. There were also snowstorms much further south. The southern state of Louisiana had 100mm of snow – its highest snowfall for 15 years. In Arkansas, ice storms linked to the blizzards cut electricity supplies to thousands of homes for nine days.

In central areas of the USA, cold dense air travelling from the north meets warm, moist air travelling up from the Gulf of Mexico, creating several climatic hazards. The warm moist air is lifted up quite violently as the cold denser air undercuts it. As it rises, the moist air condenses and forms huge cumulonimbus clouds, creating thunderstorms and lightning. Hailstones are also common, formed when raindrops caught in the rapidly rising air freeze and fall. Some hailstones can be as big as golf balls and can completely flatten large areas of crops.

TORNADOES

Tornadoes are caused by similar conditions to those that cause thunderstorms, but with the addition of a fast-moving upper air stream. The upper air stream turns the warm rising air and a revolving funnel is created. At ground level this tornado (or 'twister') destroys everything in its path. Tornadoes can be up to a kilometre wide, but are usually less than 100m wide, with winds of up to 500km per hour. Tornado Alley is the name given to an area over Texas, Oklahoma, Kansas and Nebraska, where most of the large destructive tornadoes occur (see map on page 17). In April 2001 six people were killed in tornadoes in Mississippi and Arkansas, on the edge of Tornado Alley, and over 300 homes were damaged.

Abandoned cars in Buffalo, New York state, after an unexpected snowstorm in November 2000.

CASE STUDY
HURRICANE FLOYD, SEPTEMBER 1999

In September 1999 Hurricane Floyd formed in the mid-Atlantic, off the east coast of the USA. At first, observers predicted it would come ashore in Florida, and an evacuation of 2 million coastal residents was organised – the largest evacuation in the history of the USA. However, Hurricane Floyd bypassed Florida and on 16 September came ashore in North Carolina instead. Although winds with speeds up to 160km per hour caused considerable wind damage, it was the torrential rain that caused most of the damage. Over 500mm of rain fell in just 12 hours. After the worst of the hurricane had passed, the rivers rose rapidly and there was serious flooding. The majority of the 35 deaths in North Carolina were due to drowning. Water supplies in the area were contaminated by waste from farms and damaged sewers, as well as by the carcasses of thousands of drowned pigs and chickens. Thousands of people were made homeless and the estimated cost of the damage was US$6 billion. Once over the land Hurricane Floyd soon weakened, although heavy rains and gale-force winds were experienced by much of the north-east of the USA.

In an old forest in the Cascade Mountains of Washington, logging machinery moves harvested logs.

RAW MATERIALS

The USA is rich in natural resources and is one of the top world producers of minerals, such as aluminium, copper and lead. There are also large deposits of coal, natural gas, petroleum and uranium. Most of the metals, including copper, are mined in the western states. In 2001, the USA produced 16 per cent of the world's sulphur, most of which comes from the coastal areas of Louisiana and Texas.

Although the USA produces large amounts of minerals, it also imports several, such as zinc and silver, because it cannot produce enough to meet its own demand. The metals and minerals are used in a wide range of manufacturing industries. Sulphur is used in the manufacture of sulphuric acid and zinc is used in batteries.

Just under a third of the USA is forested and, of this amount, two-thirds is used as a timber resource, where trees are logged and sold. Softwoods such as pine are found mainly in the western coastal states, with hardwoods such as oak located more in southern states such as Georgia and North Carolina. Although sawn timber is important in the building industry (most American houses are timber-framed), most timber is used as pulp for paper manufacturing.

CASE STUDY
FORESTS OF THE PACIFIC NORTH-WEST

The western states of Washington and Oregon are famous for their evergreen forests, which consist mainly of coniferous trees such as the Douglas fir. Over 80 per cent of these forests have been felled for timber. Of the remaining areas, only 20 per cent is protected. Since these are ancient forests and an increasingly rare habitat, they need further protection. But there is conflict between conservationists and the logging industry. The US government has forbidden any more felling of the older areas of forest to protect the northern spotted owl, whose habitat is this ancient forest. The government's ban has had a damaging impact on local economies. In one local county in Oregon, after the owl was declared an endangered species in 1990, its annual timber-industry income fell from $12.7–$2.1 million. Overall it was estimated that 100,000 jobs were lost in the north-west as a result of protecting the owl and its habitat. Loggers put stickers on their cars saying, 'If it's hooting, I'm shooting!'

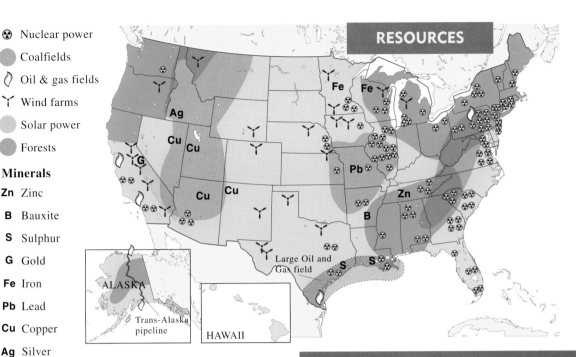

Key:

- ☢ Nuclear power
- Coalfields
- ⬭ Oil & gas fields
- Ⴤ Wind farms
- Solar power
- Forests

Minerals

- **Zn** Zinc
- **B** Bauxite
- **S** Sulphur
- **G** Gold
- **Fe** Iron
- **Pb** Lead
- **Cu** Copper
- **Ag** Silver

ALASKA

Trans-Alaska pipeline

HAWAII

Large Oil and Gas field

US PRODUCTION OF METALS (% OF WORLD TOTAL), 2001

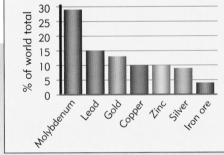

Source: US Statistical Abstract, 2003

CASE STUDY
COPPER MINING AT BINGHAM

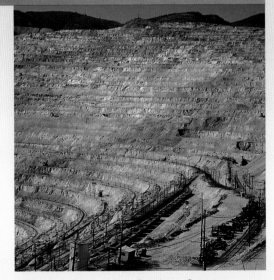

The open-cast mine at Bingham Canyon.

Since 1998, copper production in the USA has reduced due to low world demand, and some mines in the USA have had to close. The copper mine at Bingham Canyon, in Utah, is the largest human excavation in the world.

Its huge size makes it still worthwhile to mine there. The mine was modernised in the early 1990s to comply with new environmental laws, and a new smelter was built. Almost all (99.9 per cent) of the sulphur produced in the smelting process is now captured by a new smelter. If the sulphur was allowed to escape it could form sulphur dioxide, which is a major ingredient in acid rain. The waste heat produced by the smelting process is recycled to generate power. Restoration work has been carried out on the old mine dumps and the mining company has won an environmental award for its care of the landscape. The mine has a workforce of over 2,000 people and pays total annual wages of $50 million. Property taxes paid by the mine help the local economy even more.

ENERGY

The USA has 5 per cent of the world's population, yet it uses 40 per cent of the world's fossil fuel production. The average American family has a high standard of living that depends on fuel for at least two cars, heating in winter, and electricity to run air-conditioning in the summer and a large number of appliances in the home. This means a huge demand for energy.

In April 2001 power cuts in California were caused by a drought in Washington state. Low flow in the rivers meant less hydroelectric power (HEP) was produced and there was no surplus to send to California. Many Americans began to look at alternative sources of energy.

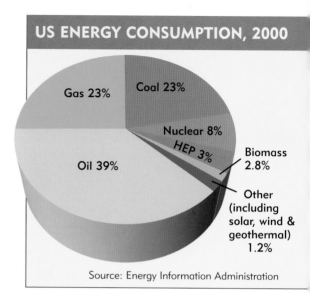

US ENERGY CONSUMPTION, 2000

Gas 23%
Coal 23%
Nuclear 8%
HEP 3%
Biomass 2.8%
Oil 39%
Other (including solar, wind & geothermal) 1.2%

Source: Energy Information Administration

COAL

The USA is the world's second-biggest producer of coal after China. In 1999 there were about 1,800 coal mines in the east, the Rocky Mountains and the northern Great Plains. The leading coal-producing state is Wyoming, where the industry produces 31 per cent of the USA's total production and employs nearly 5,000 people. The coal produced is low in sulphur and ash, so it burns more cleanly than coal from other areas.

Most mining is by open-cast methods and in some cases the coal is loaded automatically on to trains and sent directly to power stations. As coal is removed from the ground the landscape is restored, and grasses and trees are planted.

NUCLEAR POWER

In 2004, nuclear reactors produced 20 per cent of the USA's electricity. There were concerns about its safety and no new nuclear power stations were planned. Between 2000 and 2001 the percentage of people in favour of

An open-cast coal mine in Gillette, Wyoming.

nuclear power in the USA rose from 45–66 per cent. Compared to coal-burning power stations, nuclear power is a cleaner type of fuel because it does not release carbon dioxide, which contributes towards global warming. Several new nuclear power stations are now planned.

However, one of the problems linked to nuclear power is the storage of radioactive waste. At Yucca Mountain, 140km north of Las Vegas, there is conflict between Native American communities and the nuclear power industry. The industry wants to create a huge underground nuclear dump beneath the mountain. The Native Americans are worried that the waste will contaminate water supplies. Since the waste will take 10,000 years to become safe, it is a long-term problem.

RENEWABLE ENERGY

The USA has developed a wide range of renewable energy sources, including geothermal, wave, biomass, solar, wind and HEP. Solar power is becoming more popular in the warmer states, such as Florida and California. Solar 'farms' in the desert areas of California use huge banks of solar cells to convert the sun's energy into power. Since California's power cuts in April 2001, people have been paying to have solar panels put on their roofs to reduce their electricity bills and give them an alternative energy supply.

Biomass power includes landfill gas sites. Biomass power provides 2.8 per cent of the

Large-scale wind farms, such as this one in California, provide Americans with an alternative power source to fossil fuels.

USA's energy. Timber waste is also used as a fuel for some power stations.

Hydroelectric power is important on many of the USA's rivers. The largest HEP plant is at the Grand Coulee Dam on the Columbia River, in Washington state. Usually, 75 per cent of the electricity produced is sold outside the state, unless drought reduces production.

Wind energy in California provides 95 per cent of the country's total wind power, yet this is only 1.5 per cent of the state's total power needs. This amount is 30 per cent of the world's total wind energy production. New, large-scale wind farms across California use massive wind turbines to produce electricity.

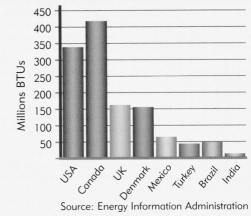

AVERAGE ENERGY CONSUMPTION PER PERSON, 2002

Source: Energy Information Administration

OIL AND GAS

The USA has the twelfth-largest oil reserves in the world, producing 5.7 million barrels of crude oil per day, plus large amounts of natural gas. Yet only 43 per cent of the country's needs are met by its own oil wells. The rest has to be imported. The country consumes 26 per cent of the world's available oil, but with only 5 per cent of its population. It is estimated that by 2025, the USA's population will be greater than 300 million and only 15 per cent of its own oil will remain untapped.

The USA depends heavily on oil for transport and industry. Its size and its limited public transport means there are not many alternatives to the car. At present, Americans pay less for their petrol than Europeans and the government is reluctant to increase the price. But low oil prices are making it difficult for oil companies to survive, and many companies are merging so they can afford to explore and develop new oil fields.

The government has an emergency stockpile of 570 million barrels of oil stored in caverns along the Gulf of Mexico coast. In September 2000, some was released to cover a possible shortage of heating fuel for the winter.

The majority of oil is found within four states: Texas, Alaska, California and Louisiana.

TEXAS

The state of Texas produces 26 per cent of the USA's oil, and still has large reserves. Production peaked in 1972, but since then, even with new discoveries, it is continuing to decline. Most of the new oil and gas wells are in the Gulf of Mexico. New technology means that offshore wells can now be sunk in deep water to tap the reserves.

Pipes raised above the snow carry oil to a collection centre in Alaska.

US OIL CONSUMPTION AND CRUDE OIL PRODUCTION, 1990–2003

Source: Texas Petrofacts; Energy Information Administration

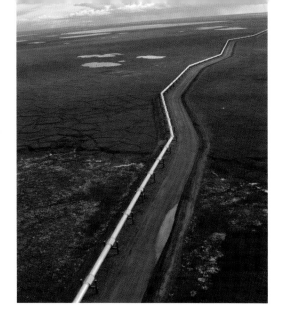

The Trans-Alaska oil pipeline at Prudhoe Bay, Alaska. The pipeline carries oil from the bay to the port at Valdez.

ALASKA

Alaska produces 17 per cent of the USA's oil, with most coming from the Prudhoe Bay field in north Alaska. Prudhoe Bay is a port, but it is covered in ice for much of the year, so the oil is warmed and pumped through a pipeline to the southern Alaskan port of Valdez. The pipeline is 1,280km long. It crosses three

mountain ranges and nearly 800 rivers and streams before reaching Valdez, where oil is loaded on to tankers from the pipeline. For 672km, the pipeline is above ground because of the difficulties of burying it in frozen soil. The sections above ground follow a zig-zag path to allow the pipe to expand and contract, and to allow it to move during an earthquake. Some parts of the pipeline are over 3m above ground to allow herds of caribou to migrate underneath. Under rivers, the pipeline has to be insulated to prevent the warm oil thawing the ground, which might then sink, so allowing oil to escape into the environment, damaging the fragile tundra vegetation.

OIL SPILL

One of the USA's worst oil spills occurred in 1989 when a tanker, the *Exxon Valdez*, ran aground near the port of Valdez, spilling 37,000 tonnes of oil. It caused an environmental disaster, coating much of the coastline in oil and killing fish, sea otters and other animals. Today the area has largely recovered, but it is still being monitored.

CASE STUDY
ARCTIC NATIONAL WILDLIFE REFUGE

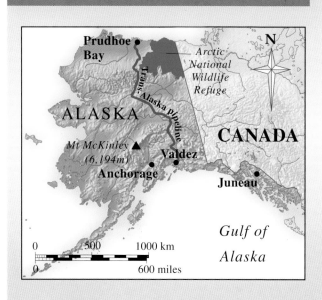

The Arctic National Wildlife Refuge is an area within Alaska that has, until now, been protected from oil exploration and development. Part of the reserve is thought to have oil deposits. If oil wells are dug in the area, only 10 per cent of the reserve would be affected, but the oil-rich area includes most of the coastal plain, where caribou migrate and polar bears have their breeding dens. In May 2001, President Bush said that the ANWR was to be opened up to oil exploration. Even if the oil is worth recovering, it will only provide the USA with nine months' supply of its oil needs. Yet it could destroy an important wildlife refuge and interfere with the migration and breeding of the largest caribou herd on the continent.

PEOPLE OF THE USA

The USA has a diverse population, the result of many migrations of people from different parts of the world. In 2004, its population was 297 million, having grown by around 49 million since 1990. The population is a valuable resource to the country.

The original inhabitants of the USA were Native Americans, who migrated from Asia thousands of years ago. Today there are about 2 million Native Americans living in the USA, mostly in the western states. Europeans arrived in America after Christopher Columbus landed in the West Indies, in 1492. There followed settlement by the English, Spanish, Germans, French and Dutch. In the eighteenth century, black slaves were brought from Africa to the plantations of the southern states. In the nineteenth century, potato famines in Ireland triggered large migrations of Irish. Since then, there have been further waves of migration from China, southern and Eastern Europe, Latin America and Asia. Some migrants came to America to escape from religious persecution. Others came because of the chance of a better life for themselves and for their children. Today, most migrants are from Latin America, especially Mexico.

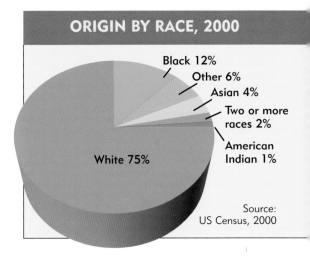

ORIGIN BY RACE, 2000

Black 12%
Other 6%
Asian 4%
Two or more races 2%
American Indian 1%
White 75%

Source: US Census, 2000

MEXICAN MIGRANTS

The USA shares a border with Mexico, and the high standard of living in the USA acts as a magnet to Mexican migrants. In 2003, the USA's GNI per head was $37,610 compared to only $6,230 in Mexico. There are few jobs in Mexico and nearly 40 per cent of the Mexican population is unemployed.

In the USA, Mexicans have traditionally been employed as seasonal agricultural workers in states such as California, where they help with planting and harvesting. Many have stayed on and become legal US citizens. In 2000 there were 21 million Mexicans living in the USA, forming nearly 8 per cent of the population. California has nearly 4 million legal Mexican

A recent immigrant from Mexico at work in a clothing factory in El Paso, Texas.

These teenagers are performing a Mexican dance at a street festival in Austin, Texas.

residents, but this number is almost matched by the number of illegal migrants. The Mexican border is patrolled by guards to stop the entry of illegal migrants. Along isolated stretches of the Rio Grande River, on the Texas-Mexico boundary, many migrants try to swim across. The migrants want decent jobs, access to health care and to be able to give their children a good education. To do this, they are willing to work hard in low-paid jobs, jobs that it is often difficult to persuade American citizens to take.

At first, Mexican migrants were concentrated in the southern states such as California and Texas, which have borders with Mexico. In 2000, for the first time in California, Spanish speakers outnumbered English speakers. Mexicans are now moving to other parts of the USA, where there is less competition for jobs. Some are even moving to Alaska to work on fishing fleets.

Mexican influence can be seen on the streets of most cities in the USA. There are Spanish-style fiestas, food shops and restaurants, as well as Spanish-language television and radio. New migrants generally want to become Americans and yet hold on to their language and culture.

US POPULATION, 1950–2050

Population (millions)

400
300
200
100

1950   1970   2000   *2015   *2050

Sources: UN Population Division; *Geographical Digest;* UNDP. *= Estimates

AGRICULTURE, INDUSTRY AND TRADE

Wheat being harvested by giant combine harvesters in the northern Great Plains.

USA is a world leader in agricultural production. In the east there is enough rainfall to support a range of crops and livestock. The soils are generally more fertile than further west. Most corn (maize) is produced between the states of Ohio and Nebraska, and between Minnesota and Missouri. A belt of cotton production stretches from South Carolina to Texas.

In the interior of the country the climate is drier and there are vast expanses of wheat production. Extensive livestock rearing is found in the mountainous and very dry areas of the west. This is the land of the cowboy and cattle herding. Much of the west coast is a mixture of forests, crops and some livestock farming. Market gardening, a form of intensive agriculture where there are very high inputs of labour and chemicals, is found close to areas of large population, such as San Francisco and Los Angeles.

Farming employs only about 2 per cent of the USA's working population. Over the last 50 years, farms have become fewer in number but much larger in size. This is because it is cheaper to run a larger farm, since chemicals, feedstuffs and fuel can be purchased at a discount for large quantities. It is cheaper to have very large fields farmed using machinery and to reduce labour costs.

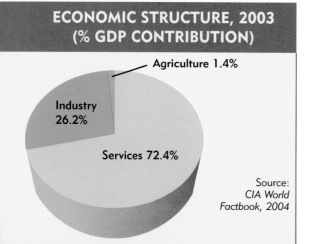

ECONOMIC STRUCTURE, 2003 (% GDP CONTRIBUTION)

Agriculture 1.4%

Industry 26.2%

Services 72.4%

Source: CIA World Factbook, 2004

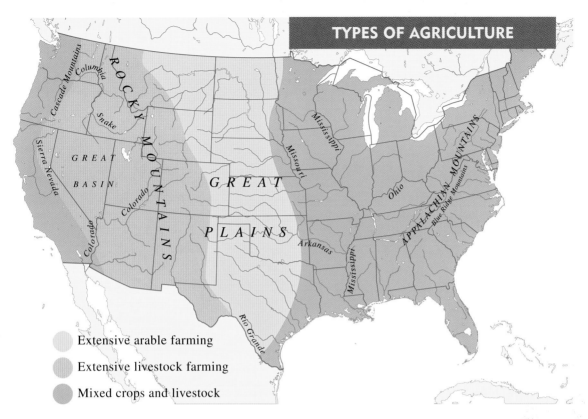

- Extensive arable farming
- Extensive livestock farming
- Mixed crops and livestock

CASE STUDY
IRRIGATED FARMING IN THE COLUMBIA BASIN

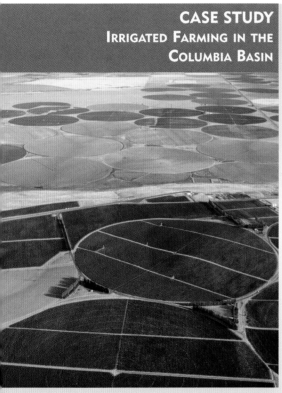

Vineyards in Washington state. The USA is one of the world's leading producers of wine.

Although western Washington has high rainfall, once inland, under the rain shadow of the Rockies, rainfall is very low. Irrigation from the Columbia River and its tributaries has made this region into a highly productive area. Washington state is the country's leading producer of apples, growing 6 billion a year and 33 per cent of the entire US crop. In the valley of the Yakima River, a tributary of the Columbia, the soil and temperatures are ideal for growing apples and many other fruits. Water is taken from the Yakima to irrigate the crops and high levels of production are achieved. All of the USA's hops (for use in beer making) are grown under irrigation in the Yakima Valley, making the country the second-largest producer of beer in the world. The world's largest-producing area of spearmint is on the Columbia Plateau. Irrigated farming is an intensive type of agriculture because of the high costs involved, particularly the cost of transporting water. Although increasingly mechanised, many of the crops still demand a large amount of labour.

A steelworks in Pittsburgh, Pennsylvania, being demolished piece by piece in 1983.

THE RUST BELT

Manufacturing first began in the USA near the Atlantic ports, but as the population moved westwards it developed in the new cities along the Great Lakes and along the navigable rivers of the region (see map on page 31). At the beginning of the twentieth century a manufacturing belt stretched from Chicago in the west to Boston, New York and Baltimore in the east. It was the most important manufacturing region in the world, especially for steel. This manufacturing belt developed and expanded because of the locally available raw materials, especially iron ore and coal, and the good transport links by water, rail and later by road. There was also access to the large markets in the east of the region.

In the second half of the twentieth century, many of the older, heavy industries in the region, such as steel-making, declined. This was partially due to competition from overseas, but also due to world overproduction of steel, which drove down its price. The region was renamed the 'rust belt'.

PITTSBURGH

Pittsburgh was, perhaps, the city most strongly linked to the steel industry. Its rivers carried in iron ore and coal, which were used to make steel. The same rivers were used to take away the finished product. By 1983 the city's economy was in decline, and 80,000 steel-making jobs had been lost over the previous year. However, the wealth created in the past had founded several good colleges and universities, which helped drive industrial change through the city.

Since the 1980s, many hi-tech firms have been attracted to Pittsburgh by tax incentives, and by having access to research and development carried out in the universities. Pittsburgh is now the fifth-largest producer of software in the USA. The loss of heavy industry has led to cleaner air and a more pleasant environment. The old steel plants along the rivers have been converted into warehouses or small business units. The city now has a more varied industrial base.

DETROIT

The city of Detroit was known as 'Mo'town' (motor town) because car manufacture used to be its main industry. Again, because of foreign competition, this industry has been in decline and there have been many job losses. But a $100-billion-scheme has been started to regenerate the economy and to try to attract new businesses. Some of the new firms are keen to use the city's highly skilled workforce. The former Cadillac assembly plant is being developed as a technology park, and should create as many as 1,700 permanent jobs when it is completed.

CHICAGO

Chicago is the main city in the rust belt. It grew because of its position on Lake Michigan, and later as the hub of many railway routes. A canal links the lake to the Mississippi River, giving access to the south of the USA. Chicago's traditional industries include meat-processing and steel-making. In the 1980s' recession most of the city's steel industries closed down, but it already had a wider industrial base than most cities. It is an

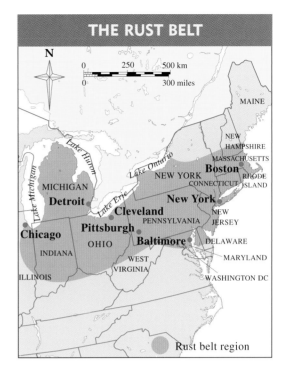

THE RUST BELT

important financial and banking centre, and has many company headquarters. In April 2001 the aeroplane company Boeing decided to move its headquarters to Chicago from Seattle, largely because of its central location.

The cities of the rust belt continue to face challenges. During the early months of 2001 there were further losses in manufacturing. But the cities are fighting to develop a more varied industrial base, and to move into the twenty-first century with a more stable, multi-industry economy.

Traders work frantically inside Chicago's giant Stock Exchange.

STRUCTURE OF INDUSTRY, PENNSYLVANIA, 2004

Mining and construction 5%

Trade, transport and utilities 20%

Manufacturing 13%

Services (including government) 62%

Source: Bureau of Labor Statistics

ABOVE: The headquarters of a large computer firm in Silicon Valley, California.

INSET: Jobs in hi-tech industries are sought after because they are usually well paid.

THE SUNBELT – BOOM OR BUST?

The Sunbelt area originally included two states, Florida and California, but it now includes other states, such as Georgia, Tennessee and Alabama, and definitions of it keep changing. These states all have a warm, sunny climate, which attracts people to live and work there. The industries that have grown in these locations are mainly hi-tech industries, not tied to the sources of raw materials. They include computer development and the production of semiconductors. These industries are known as 'footloose industries', and are typical of the new industries of the late twentieth and early twenty-first centuries. Since they are market-orientated, they are located near large centres of population where their products are sold, or close to transport routes that offer easy access to such centres.

Hi-tech industries tend to be located near universities, so they can have access to research. Flat land is required for landscaped company factories, with room for expansion. The industries generally create very little noise or pollution, and can be built near residential areas. They are usually close to airports, so it is easy to import component parts and export the finished goods.

SILICON VALLEY, CALIFORNIA

The area known as Silicon Valley lies just south of San Francisco. It is the main area within the USA for the design and production of microchips, electronic circuitry and computer software. Large numbers of firms are located

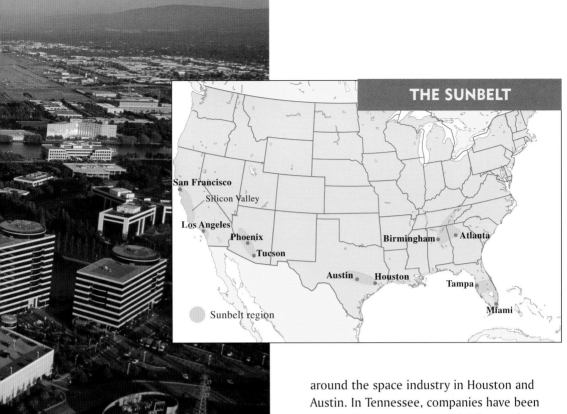

San Francisco
Silicon Valley
Los Angeles
Phoenix
Tucson
Birmingham
Atlanta
Austin
Houston
Tampa
Miami

Sunbelt region

here around Stanford University. In the 1950s the university leased some land to hi-tech companies to help raise money for expansion. Over the years more companies arrived, attracted by the university, good road routes, nearby airports, and the pleasant climate for their employees. Employees stay in each job for an average of two years in the Silicon Valley, and it is common for people to move to rival firms, or set up on their own. All employees are encouraged to think of ideas for new products, to keep their company ahead of the rest of the world in new technology.

LA, TEXAS AND TENNESSEE

Other hi-tech areas within the Sunbelt are found in Los Angeles. Here, the government's investment in the aerospace industry over the past 50 years has triggered large numbers of firms producing components. Other groups of hi-tech companies are found in Texas, based

around the space industry in Houston and Austin. In Tennessee, companies have been attracted by government subsidies, and are replacing dying industries such as coal-mining.

BUST

At the beginning of 2001, large numbers of employees in the computer industry were made redundant as a number of computer businesses failed due to the worldwide overproduction of microchips. The hi-tech industries had grown too fast. The industry is necessary to all sectors of the economy, but future growth must now be steady and carefully financed.

STRUCTURE OF INDUSTRY, CALIFORNIA, 2004

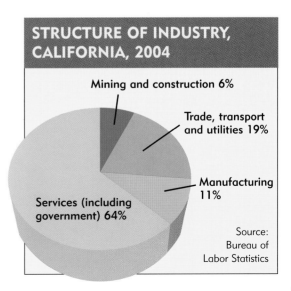

Mining and construction 6%

Trade, transport and utilities 19%

Manufacturing 11%

Services (including government) 64%

Source: Bureau of Labor Statistics

APPALACHIA – THE 'BYPASSED AREA'

Appalachia is the name of a region that covers the southern Appalachian Mountains, and includes parts of eight states. It is a poor region, made up of highlands that include the Blue Ridge and Great Smoky Mountains. These mountains were a barrier to early settlement. In the early nineteenth century, Scots, Irish, English and German settlers built small farms in the narrow river valleys. Since then there has been very little movement into or out of the region. Appalachian society is based on the family, and the local church plays an important role, often providing the social centre for a settlement.

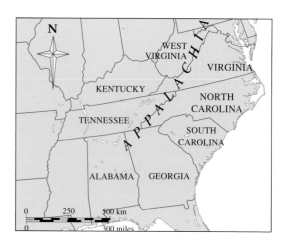

AGRICULTURE

Farms in the narrow valleys are small (about 40 hectares) and the climate can be harsh. The soils are often poor, except in the valley bottoms, and the fields are small, so it is not easy to use agricultural machinery. The farms are semi-marginal, which means they can only just support a family. Crops such as tobacco

and apples are sold, but production levels are low. Appalachian farms cannot compete with more commercial farming areas such as the Great Plains.

MINING

Huge deposits of coal lie under the plateau section of Appalachia. Until the 1980s it was used to make coke for the country's iron and steel industries, and to generate power. Its use declined in the 1980s and 1990s because Appalachian coal has a high sulphur content. The government's emission laws became stricter, so other less polluting forms of coal now are used in most power stations. The government has recently helped put new sulphur-removing technology into Appalachia's power stations, so that local coal continues to be used. A third of the mining is done using open-cast methods, which has a major impact on the landscape. Ten years ago there were 48 mining companies in the region. This has been reduced to only eight, and their future is not certain. Mechanisation has reduced the number of miners needed to work the remaining pits. Most of the profits leave the region because the companies that own the mines are based elsewhere.

GOVERNMENT HELP

The government has set up a series of initiatives to try to improve the quality of life in Appalachia. Empowerment Zones have been created to encourage private investment with

In the winter, Appalachian towns in the mountains can become isolated.

tax incentives and help with building costs. New interstate highways were built during the 1990s to reduce Appalachia's isolation and to encourage businesses to move to the region. The Federal Bureau of Investigation (FBI) moved their finger-printing facility into Appalachia, creating 2,600 local jobs. There is a small cluster of more than 70 hi-tech firms providing 1,000 jobs in the same area. Apart from a few jobs like these, most new jobs are in the low-wage sectors of service industries.

EDUCATION

The population of Appalachia is ageing, as younger people leave the region for better prospects. The percentage of students gaining High School diplomas is now higher than the national average. Young people see gaining a good diploma as a ticket out of the area, or as entry into the higher-paid, skilled jobs within the region.

TOURISM

Tourism is becoming increasingly important in Appalachia, especially in areas away from the new interstate highways. Tourists are attracted by the region's beautiful scenery and autumnal forest colours, which rival those of New England. The number of second homes being bought in the region has increased, as middle-class families in Atlanta buy cabins in the Blue Ridge Mountains for the weekends.

Appalachia still has many problems, including relatively low incomes, but its industrial base is becoming more varied and its population is now generally healthier and better educated. The 'bypassed area' has begun to join the rest of the USA.

APPALACHIA: STANDARD OF LIVING

	Appalachia	USA
Income per capita, 2000	$24,057	$29,469
Rural dwellers	44%	20%
Unemployed, 2001	5.0%	4.8%
Infant mortality per 1,000	8.3	8
Telephone owners	80%	95%

Source: US Census; Appalachian Regional Commission

Guitar and banjo players playing on the porch of the Appalachian Museum during the Tennessee Fall (autumn) Homecoming Festival.

WORLD TRADE AND AID

The USA is a wealthy and influential nation. It carries out a large amount of trade with the rest of the world, including non-democratic countries such as China. Yet its balance of trade is in the red. It imports far more than it exports, and in 2003 had a trading deficit of $541.8 billion. The trading deficit is particularly bad with Japan, where it is $66 billion. The USA's top exports include military equipment, cereals, processed foods, cars and machinery. In 2003 total

This worker at a factory in South Korea is making goods for the US company Nike.

imports were worth $1,256.3 billion. Total exports were worth $714.5 billion.

AMERICAN EXPORTS

Other important American exports are from its music, film and television industries. Disney animations and major film blockbusters are sold and seen worldwide. The USA is the home of rock music, the blues and rap, and

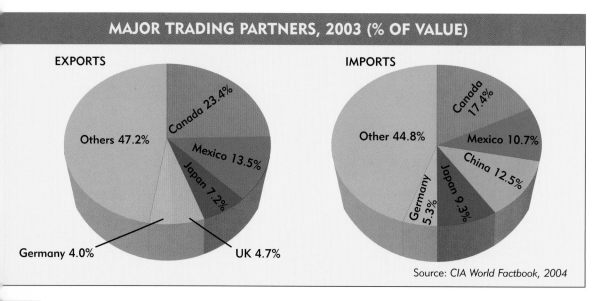

MAJOR TRADING PARTNERS, 2003 (% OF VALUE)

EXPORTS

- Canada 23.4%
- Mexico 13.5%
- Japan 7.2%
- UK 4.7%
- Germany 4.0%
- Others 47.2%

IMPORTS

- Canada 17.4%
- Mexico 10.7%
- China 12.5%
- Japan 9.3%
- Germany 5.3%
- Other 44.8%

Source: *CIA World Factbook, 2004*

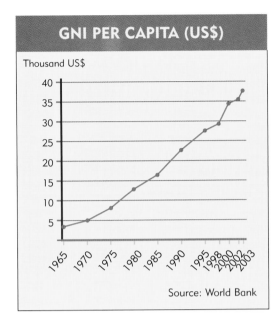

GNI PER CAPITA (US$)

Thousand US$

Source: World Bank

there is a constant flow of pop music sold around the world. Large numbers of American television programmes, especially soap operas and chat shows, are exported, and have become an integral part of the culture of many countries, including the UK and Canada.

Major American food chains are seen in towns and cities in all corners of the world. American clothing and footwear have a powerful influence because of their branding. Certain logos are recognised over much of the developed world and many people will pay a high price for them. However, many products with a US brand are not actually made in the USA. Instead they are made in countries such as Vietnam, South Korea or the Philippines, where the wages are much lower.

NATO AND THE UN

The USA is a member of many powerful world organisations, including the North Atlantic Treaty Organisation (NATO). NATO is a defence alliance consisting of the USA and 15 other countries. It was set up in 1949 to counter the influence of the communist Soviet Union. Since the end of the Cold War, former communist and socialist countries, such as Russia, have also had a voice within NATO.

The USA is also a member of the United Nations (UN). This is a group set up after the Second World War to protect human rights and the environment, and to tackle poverty in the world. The UN also has a peacekeeping role, providing troops and observers in areas of conflict, such as Bosnia and Sierra Leone. The contribution of the USA to the UN's peacekeeping funds has been calculated at 30 per cent. However, the USA feels it should only contribute 25 per cent. This is affecting the UN's ability to carry out its role in times of crisis.

AID

The USA provides funds for the development of poorer nations. This includes projects to improve agriculture, to increase childhood immunisation against diseases, to combat HIV and AIDS, and to improve the level of female literacy. However, although the USA does contribute a great deal of money to overseas aid, it is a tiny percentage of its Gross National Income (GNI). The UN recommends that developed nations donate 0.7 per cent of their GNI to aid. In 2002 the USA's contribution was only 0.12 per cent.

US troops taking part in the Gulf War against Iraq, in 1991.

A freight train makes its way across the American Midwest.

GETTING AROUND

The USA is a country of huge distances. To drive from New York in the north-east, to Los Angeles in the south-west is a journey of more than 4,000km. Transport is a major sector of the country's economy and in 2001 contributed $303 billion to the Gross Domestic Product. The industry transports raw materials and finished products as well as passengers, and it also employs large numbers of people.

RAIL

The railways originally opened up the west of the USA to settlement, but today they are not the most important form of transport. The railway network is most dense on the eastern side of the country. Only a few passenger lines cross the country. In California, more railway lines are being developed, and buses are linking areas that do not have access to a railway. This is to encourage people to leave the heavily congested roads. Between Boston and Washington DC, a high-speed rail service called the Acela Express increased its use by 10 per cent in 2001. The train travels at up to 240km per hour and offers a fast alternative to flying or going by road.

The railways are still important for transporting long-distance, heavy freight, such as coal, iron ore and timber products. The Union Pacific Railroad is one of the largest freight carriers and serves the 23 western states. It links every major West Coast and Gulf Coast port. Many freight trains carry large amounts of a single type of freight, which keeps costs down. The amount of rail freight is increasing because the fuel costs of moving large quantities can be much lower than transporting by road.

AIR TRAVEL

For travel within the USA, many people choose to fly rather than go by road. There are over 5,000 airports in the country. In 2003 the busiest airport was Atlanta in Georgia, a gateway airport to other flight journeys, which had 79 million passengers.

WATER TRANSPORT

Water transport is important for carrying goods. The Great Lakes link the industrial

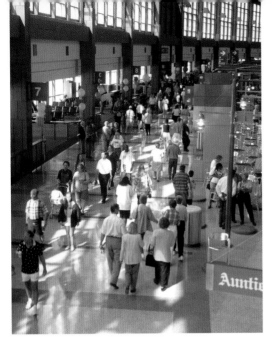

Passengers in the terminal building at Austin-Bergstrom International Airport in Austin, Texas.

cars and 92 million trucks (including people carriers, pick-ups and 4x4s). The country has a system of interstate highways, with wide, well-maintained roads between major cities and across the country. They are used by the trucking industry and carry a great deal of freight. For much of the country there is no alternative to the car because very few places have access to a railway. Public transport such as the New York Subway is only well-developed in areas with a high population density. At present, only 5 per cent of the US population use public transport.

Problems with such a heavy dependency on the car include poor air quality, heavy traffic congestion and a rapidly decreasing oil supply. Car journey times are increasing, but are still shorter than the average time taken when using public transport.

The USA needs to find alternatives to such a heavy dependence on the car as an individual form of transport. One suggestion is the use of fully automated highway systems that are currently being tested in Japan. Here, groups of cars are computer-controlled on the motorways so that more traffic can be carried at any one time. The control systems are in charge of accelerating, braking, and distances between vehicles. They may be one solution to the congested freeways of cities like Los Angeles.

cities on their shores to the Atlantic Ocean, and ocean-going vessels can move between them. The USA has many important ports, the most important being South Louisiana, at the mouth of the Mississippi. In 2003 the port dealt with 3,753 ships and 53,953 barges. It links the Gulf of Mexico to the inland barge system via the Mississippi, and gives access to 31,000km of inland waterway.

ROAD TRANSPORT

The majority of transport in the USA is by road. In 2001 there were nearly 138 million

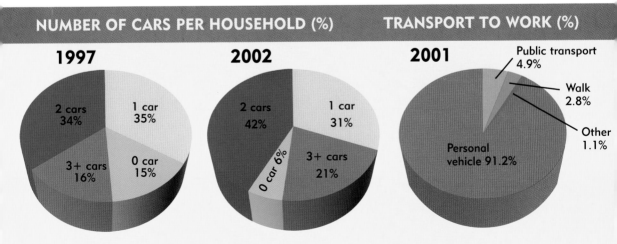

NUMBER OF CARS PER HOUSEHOLD (%)

1997
- 2 cars 34%
- 1 car 35%
- 3+ cars 16%
- 0 car 15%

2002
- 2 cars 42%
- 1 car 31%
- 0 car 6%
- 3+ cars 21%

TRANSPORT TO WORK (%)

2001
- Public transport 4.9%
- Walk 2.8%
- Other 1.1%
- Personal vehicle 91.2%

Sources: US Census; Bureau of Transportation Statistics; National Household Travel Survey

URBANISATION

The USA is now a largely urban country, with 75 per cent of the population living in towns and cities. The fastest urban growth is mainly in the south and west of the country.

The USA's earliest settlements were established along the Atlantic coast by European settlers in the seventeenth century. The coastal plain was fairly flat, which made settlement easy. Ships brought manufactured goods to the ports and took away furs, timber and crops. Some sites, such as Boston and New York, also had the advantage of being at the mouths of rivers. This helped send goods via the rivers further inland, where other towns developed.

Over the eighteenth and nineteenth centuries these eastern cities continued to grow, as industries developed based on goods flowing through their ports. In the nineteenth century, railways made links between cities much faster than by water. Some cities, such as Chicago, grew because they were situated where several railway lines converged.

BOSTON AND THE EAST

In the twentieth century, five cities continued to grow in the east: Boston, New York, Philadelphia, Baltimore and Washington DC. These five large urban areas merged to form an extensive, largely urbanised landscape, stretching from Boston down to Washington DC. This is called Boswash. It is a megalopolis.

EARLY IMMIGRATION

Boston was settled by early immigrants from England in 1630. The site was mainly flat, with low hills at the centre. There was a good water supply and easy access to water transport. Boston's early wealth came from trade with Europe. Banks and financial institutions were set up to support the trade. Processing industries such as flour-milling grew up. At the end of the nineteenth century a wide range of manufacturing was carried out, including textiles and shipbuilding.

Manhattan Island, New York City, is surrounded by four rivers, including the East River on its eastern border and the Hudson on its west. This photo was taken before 11 September 2001, when the twin towers of the World Trade Center (on the left of the picture) were destroyed by terrorists.

Several waves of migrants came to Boston to work in the expanding industries, including Italians, who arrived from 1870. Italian culture still dominates some areas of the city.

INDUSTRIAL CHANGE

The twentieth century saw the decline of many of Boston's traditional industries, although clothing and leather industries still remain. Most goods are now taken away by road or rail, or shipped out through the port of New York City. Boston is still important as a financial and academic centre, and it has seen the rise of hi-tech industries, clustered along Route 128. One of the main reasons for their location in Boston is its links to Harvard University and the Massachusetts Institute of Technology (MIT).

Tourism is becoming increasingly important for the city because of its many links with the nation's early history. Parts of central Boston, such as Beacon Hill, look more European than American, with their narrow, cobbled streets and small houses.

CONGESTION

One of Boston's problems is traffic congestion. The main six-lane elevated highway through the city is jammed for at least seven hours a day. A project is underway, called 'The Big Dig', which involves building an underground, eight-lane expressway to replace the elevated highway. Tunnels are also to be built, to give Boston new links with its airport. The Big Dig is due to be completed in 2004 and will improve central Boston's landscape and air quality. It will also create 60 hectares of open space and parks.

Boston's population is still growing, its hi-tech industries continue to develop and it is attracting more and more young professionals to live and work there. Older areas of the city have been redeveloped to improve conditions, with many attractive waterfront locations. The city is still important for banking and finance which, along with hi-tech industries, tourism and the remaining traditional industries, give Boston a sound foundation for the future.

The entrance to one of the huge road tunnels that are being built as part of 'The Big Dig' in Boston, Massachusetts.

URBAN POPULATION GROWTH, 1950–2015

Source: *Geographical Digest*; UNDP
*= estimate

The first hotels were constructed in the 1940s. Today there are huge casino hotels offering an ever-wider range of shows and entertainment, as well as constant access to gaming tables and slot machines.

Las Vegas attracts huge numbers of tourists all year round. An increasing number of people want to move to the city to live, attracted by the bright lights, the dry desert atmosphere and by the fact that it has no state income tax.

PROBLEMS OF GROWTH

The growth of Las Vegas has caused problems. The city suffers from air pollution from the increasingly heavy traffic flows, and traffic jams are common at all times of the day. There is not enough water for the increasing population and, as water is extracted from aquifers beneath the city, the land is sinking.

The urban sprawl of Los Angeles covers a vast area, linked together by freeways.

LOS ANGELES, LAS VEGAS AND THE NEW URBANISATION

Los Angeles grew massively in the twentieth century, with a population reaching 3.7 million by 2002. It became the USA's second-biggest city after New York. Los Angeles' original growth was based on agriculture, particularly its citrus groves. Later growth was due to the development of its oil, film and aerospace industries. Today, the city continues to attract people because of its climate and lifestyle. Its low-density suburbs have spread out into the desert, earning Los Angeles the name of 'Sixty-Mile City'.

LAS VEGAS

The USA's fastest-growing city is Las Vegas, the gambling capital of the world. In 1990 its population was 258,000. By 2003 it had grown to 517,000. The city was founded in the desert in 1904 with the development of the railway. It made an ideal stopping point in the desert because of the springs found there.

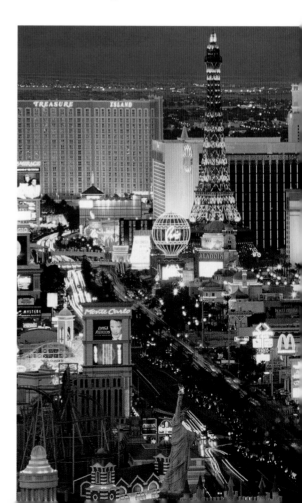

More suburbs are being built out in the desert, placing increased stress on the water supplies, roads, schools and other services of the city. The citizens of Las Vegas are deciding whether their city should be allowed to continue to grow at its present rate.

GATED COMMUNITIES

At the end of the twentieth century, urban developments called gated communities were established. Several are found in Florida. Here, people buy a house within a community, where the only access is via a barrier manned by a guard. The whole housing complex is walled. Often, these communities are dominated by the over-60-year-olds, who are worried about crime and feel secure within this type of development.

The main street of Las Vegas, the gambling capital of the USA.

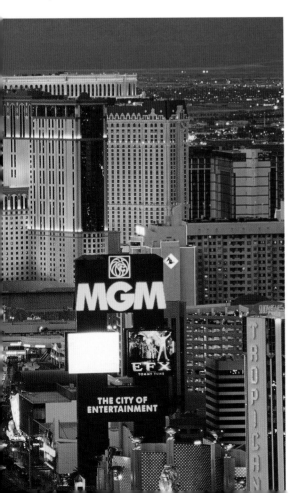

As America continues to urbanise, problems such as crime rates, traffic congestion and poor air quality have been carried into the twenty-first century. Future growth of its cities is being questioned and alternatives to growth are being researched.

CASE STUDY
CELEBRATION, FLORIDA

One of the streets in Celebration, a town built by the Disney Corporation.

Celebration, in Florida, is a new town that has been planned and developed by the Walt Disney Company. It is not a theme park but a real community based on what a small town would have been like in America 50 years ago. It is not gated, but people who live in Celebration must abide by certain rules. Only certain colours can be used to paint the fronts of their houses. Shrubs in their gardens must not be too large. Already, the early residents feel that the community is taking shape. There is a school, a bank, shops and a hospital. Residents have the use of electric vehicles to get around the town, which are less polluting than petrol-driven motors. All amenities are designed to be within walking distance of peoples' homes. The crime rate is very low and residents say that this is a reflection of the community spirit found in the town.

PEOPLE AND CULTURE

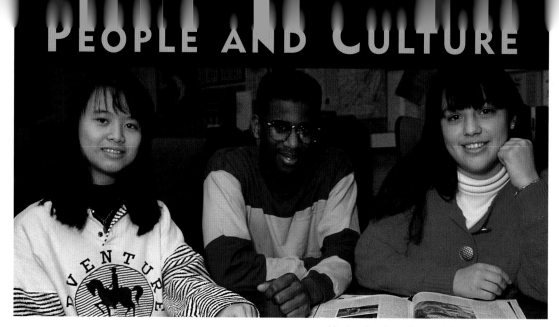

High school students of Asian, African and European origins studying together.

THE AMERICAN FAMILY

Although there are areas of great poverty within the USA, the average standard of living is high. About 99 per cent of households have a television and 55 per cent of children have a television in their bedrooms. Each person watches an average of five hours of television a day. Families eat out frequently, and there are many chains of restaurants that offer reasonably priced family meals. Most teenagers expect to learn to drive at the age of 16, and hope to have their own car.

AVERAGE AMERICAN FAMILY

Average household size with children	3.21
Infant mortality per 1,000 births	8
Life expectancy	77 years
Average annual family income before tax	$49,430
Age of consent	16
Age able to hold a driving licence	16
Average number of TVs per household	2.4
Average number of cars per household	2.0

Sources: US Census; UNICEF; WHO; *American Factfinder*; Consumer Expenditure Survey, Bureau of Labor Statistics

TYPICAL AMERICAN HOUSES

Most children are born in the suburbs. The average family house has three to four bedrooms with at least two bathrooms, and several telephones and televisions. The fridge is large because food shopping is not done every day so it needs to be stored. Food is bought in large supermarkets in shopping complexes within the suburb. Nearly all houses in the USA are timber-framed, but they may have a brick surface. Most suburban houses have a lawn at the front and an enclosed garden at the back (the backyard).

SCHOOL

In a typical American family, both parents are likely to work outside the home, driving their cars to work. Children go to a nursery, or kindergarten, from an early age while their parents are at work.

Nursery costs are high and use up much of one of the two household incomes. Schooling is free and funded by each state. There are 12 grades, covering the ages six to 18. Elementary School covers Grades 1 to 6 and Junior High School covers Grades 7 to 9. Then, at the age of 15, students move to Senior High School for the last three grades. Students can leave school at 16, but few do since it is difficult to get a decent job without having completed High School. At 18 years old, students are awarded their High School Diploma and graduate from school with a formal ceremony.

COLLEGE

After High School many students study for a degree, for which they are expected to study a range of subjects. Most go to their local college, where the fees are cheaper and they can live at home. After two years, students are awarded an Associate Degree. If they go on to the state university for a further two years, they will gain a BA or BSc degree. Private universities such as Harvard, Yale and Princeton are members of the 'Ivy League', the top universities in the USA.

FIRST JOB AND MARRIAGE

The first job for American graduates often means moving to a city, where they will share

LIFE EXPECTANCY AT BIRTH

Source: WHO; UNICEF SOWC 2004

a flat with other graduates. Their jobs will give them the average American holiday of a maximum of two weeks per year.

Marriage is declining in the USA, but more and more couples are living together. The average age for marriage is about 26 years old. Families look for a house and garden in the suburbs because of the lower crime rate and the community feel.

HEALTH AND THE ELDERLY

There is no nationwide social service in the USA, and very limited welfare provision. Families are expected to save or to pay for insurance to cover times when they are old or ill.

Many elderly people move to states such as Florida, where the weather is good all year round. Sometimes, older people live in housing estates with people of a similar age, where there is a high level of security provision. Others choose to live in small houses or flats near their families. There is a wide range of activities and societies designed especially for the elderly. The over-65s are a powerful group in the USA because of their increasing numbers. By 2025, 20 per cent of the population will be over 65 and will want to have more of a say in how American society is run.

UNDER-FIVE MORTALITY RATE

Deaths per thousand births

Sources: UNICEF SOWC 2004, except 1970 from UNDP (HDR99) and 1980 from World Bank

LEISURE

Americans generally work longer hours than Europeans, and spend an average of eight hours a week travelling to and from work. This means the time available for leisure activities is on average only 20 hours a week. Employers often demand that their employees take their two weeks' annual holiday separately, so that their work is not disrupted. This means that Americans have to carefully plan their limited leisure time.

Reading is the most popular leisure activity, and 62 per cent of adult Americans buy a daily newspaper. There are over 3,000 newspapers published in the USA. Only two have a national coverage, *USA Today* and *The Washington Post*. The others cover local or state news. There are about 10,000 magazines, some of which have huge numbers of readers. The most popular magazine – *Modern Maturity* – is aimed at retired people and has a circulation of 21 million copies.

Television is popular with all the family. There are 16 main channels plus many more local ones. The Public Broadcasting Channel (PBS) is run by the government. It shows documentaries, discussion programmes and drama.

Most socialising is based around the family, although going out for a meal is an everyday event since it is relatively cheap. Barbecues are popular, with many houses having one built into their backyard. In warmer parts of

PERSONAL COMPUTERS

Source: World Bank

the USA, where swimming pools are common, pool parties are combined with the barbecue. Alcohol cannot be served to anyone under the age of 21 in the USA. City bars serve a range of customers, but small-town bars tend to have mainly male customers.

SPORT

Sport is popular as a spectator activity but also one in which people take part. Baseball, basketball and American football are favourite American sports. Every county has a baseball league and each major city has a

American football is one of the country's favourite sports, alongside basketball and baseball.

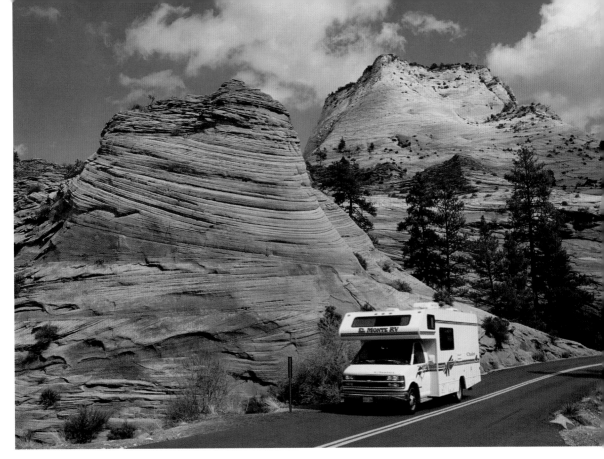

A 'recreational vehicle' (RV) winds its way through the Zion National Park in Utah.

team that competes at a national level. There are many amateur teams, and baseball games are family affairs.

Outdoor activities are also popular, with 42 per cent of Americans taking part in at least one. Walking is the favourite activity, followed by swimming. National parks are the most popular outdoor destination, with 46 per cent of Americans having visited at least one during the last 12 months.

CAMPING

Another favourite activity is to go camping at the weekend. Many families hire or own a Recreational Vehicle (RV), which is a large camper van, usually about 5–6m in length. Inside RVs are well-equipped with air-conditioning, a kitchen, bathroom and wardrobe space. RVs can often be seen on the road in the USA, towing a large car or four-wheel-drive vehicle behind them, ready for use once the RV reaches a camping ground.

Camping is also popular for holidays. America is such a vast country that many families do not even leave their state to go on holiday, and only about 20 per cent of the population goes abroad. The most popular destinations are Canada and Mexico, which border the USA. If money wasn't a restriction, the most popular choice of destination would be Australia, followed closely by the UK.

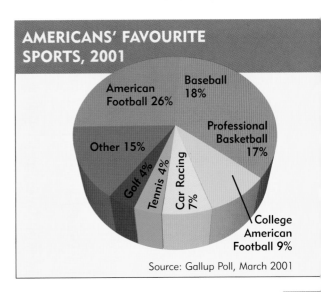

AMERICANS' FAVOURITE SPORTS, 2001

American Football 26%
Baseball 18%
Professional Basketball 17%
Other 15%
Golf 4%
Tennis 4%
Car Racing 7%
College American Football 9%

Source: Gallup Poll, March 2001

TOURISM IN THE USA

Tourism brings a great deal of money into the USA. In 2002 foreign visitors spent nearly $66.5 billion, and almost 10 million jobs are dependent on the tourist industry. Worldwide, the USA is the third most-popular tourism destination (after France and Spain). In 2002, 42 million visitors travelled to the USA.

Visitors to the USA have an enormous range of cities and landscapes from which to choose. They can visit specialist cities like Las Vegas, which is based on gambling, or New Orleans, where they can still see the influence of the French. They can visit cultural centres, such as Boston, New York City and Atlanta.

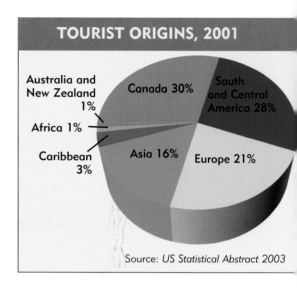

TOURIST ORIGINS, 2001

Australia and New Zealand 1%
Canada 30%
South and Central America 28%
Africa 1%
Caribbean 3%
Asia 16%
Europe 21%

Source: *US Statistical Abstract 2003*

CASE STUDY
NEW YORK CITY

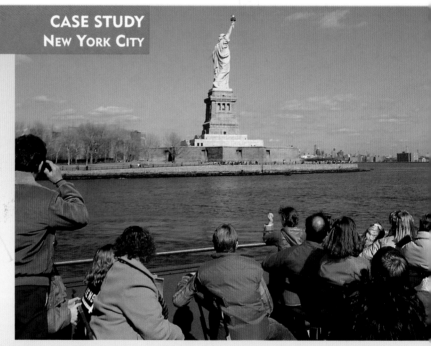

Tourists take photographs of the Statue of Liberty, from a boat in New York Harbour.

New York City is the most popular city destination for both foreign and domestic tourists. The 'Big Apple', as it is known, is a huge city with a population of 7.9 million people. Most of the sights of New York lie within Manhattan Island, including the famous Central Park. The city has many historical sights, including Ellis Island, via which many millions of immigrants entered the USA. Most visitors want to see the Statue of Liberty, which stands on Liberty Island and dominates New York harbour.

There are many important museums in the city, such as the Museum of Modern Art (MOMA). Theatres are found in the district centred on Broadway. Carnegie Hall, an important venue for music, is also found here.

Major sporting events take place in Madison Square Garden.

New York City is multicultural, with many areas of the city reflecting the homelands of immigrants. Areas of the city such as Chinatown, Little Ukraine and Little India preserve styles from different cultures.

Many visitors are attracted by the country's varied and diverse landscapes, from the desert areas of the south-west, through the rolling, grassy plains of the central states, the mountain scenery of the Rocky Mountains, the sub-tropical areas around Florida to the islands of Hawaii.

There are many opportunities for sports. Aspen, in Colorado, is a major ski resort. Watersports of all types can be undertaken along many of the coastal stretches of the USA and on the inland lakes. Some of these lakes, such as Lake Powell, are artificial. Lake Powell was created behind the Glen Canyon Dam on the Colorado River.

Florida is the most popular destination for Americans in their own country. This state has excellent beaches combined with a variety of theme parks. Las Vegas is a favourite amongst adult couples.

CASE STUDY
MONUMENT VALLEY

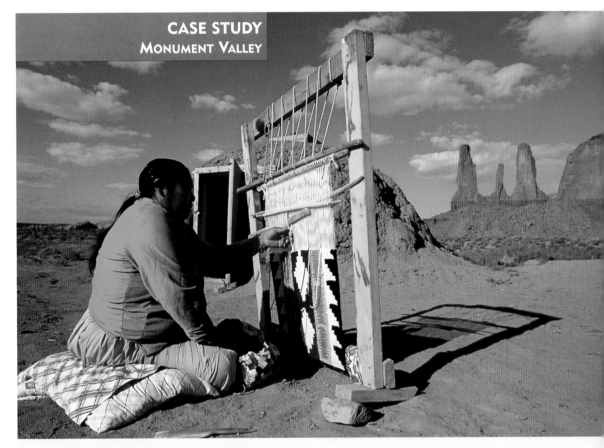

A Navajo woman weaves a traditional blanket for tourists, in Monument Valley.

Monument Valley is on the Arizona/Utah border. It is owned and managed by the Navajo, a group of Native Americans. There are about 400,000 visitors a year to this valley. It was named after its 'monuments', sandstone spires and arches, and the remnants of volcanoes. These landforms are set in a sandy desert landscape, which has been the backdrop for many cowboy films and numerous advertisements. Visitors can hire jeeps with Navajo drivers to take them on a trek around this spectacular and sacred land. As well as guiding tourists, the Navajo make and sell silver jewellery and Native American crafts.

Visitors explore the Everglades National Park, Florida, in an airboat.

NATIONAL PARKS

The USA's national parks are an important way of protecting special or vulnerable landscapes, their wildlife and history. They are also a valuable part of the tourist industry. The world's first national park was formed in the USA in 1872, at Yellowstone in Wyoming. The aim of this first park was to protect the landscape and preserve it for future generations. Today, there are 57 national parks covering a wide range of landscapes, from the tundra and forests of Alaska to the desert and sandstone arches of Utah.

National parks are an important resource to Americans because they can be used for outdoor recreation, to get away from the stresses of a mainly urban life. Towards the end of the twentieth century, their popularity resulted in increased pressures on the roads and amenities within some national parks, especially those within a few hours of large centres of population. Many parks have problems of overcrowding at certain times of the year. They are now working on ways to attract tourists outside the busiest months, to even the flow of visitors.

CASE STUDY
THE GRAND CANYON NATIONAL PARK

The Grand Canyon National Park is perhaps the most spectacular national park in the USA. It also has world importance and has been designated as a World Heritage Site. The national park is in northern Arizona, and consists of a deep, steep-walled canyon made up of many different layers of rock, with the Colorado River flowing at its base. The river flows more than 1.5km below the rim of the canyon. A descent of the canyon passes through four different vegetation zones. To encounter the same range you would need to travel from Canada to the state of New Mexico, a distance of nearly 2,000km! A former US president said of the Grand Canyon that it was 'the one great sight every American... should see.'

Most visitors come to the Grand Canyon's South Rim, which is open all year round. Facilities here include restaurants, shops, toilets, visitor centres and campsites. The large numbers of visitors mean that on a summer day there can be 6,000 vehicles trying to drive along the South Rim. This number is three times the number of parking places available and it leads to long queues and pollution from idling car engines. In summer, pollution is also blown into the park from Los Angeles, and can cause the wonderful view of the Canyon to be obscured by haze. Visitors to the Grand Canyon are in danger of 'loving it to death.'

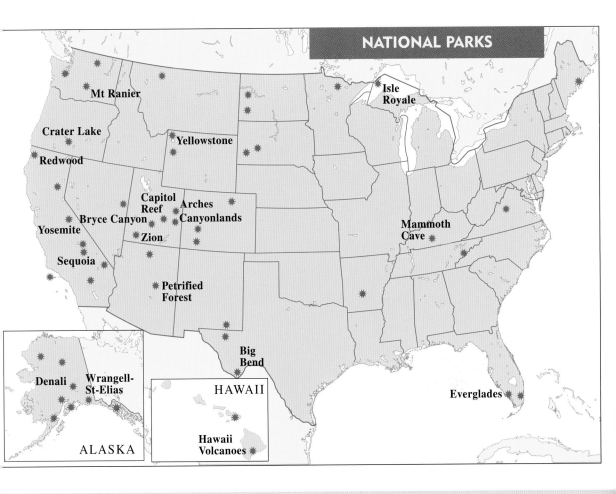

NATIONAL PARKS

Mt Ranier

Crater Lake

Yellowstone

Redwood

Capitol
Reef

Arches

Bryce Canyon

Canyonlands

Yosemite

Zion

Mammoth
Cave

Sequoia

Petrified
Forest

Isle
Royale

Big
Bend

Denali

Wrangell-
St-Elias

HAWAII

Everglades

ALASKA

Hawaii
Volcanoes

The National Park Service has taken the following steps to protect the park from human impact:

- The West Rim can only be accessed by shuttle bus.

- There is a park-and-ride system in the nearest town to the Canyon.

- A new public transport system is planned for within the park.

- Flights over the Canyon are limited in certain areas because of noise frightening the animals.

- Rangers give talks to make people aware of their impacts on the Canyon.

By carrying out these developments the National Park Service aims to ensure that the Grand Canyon remains in its natural state for future generations.

The deep, water-cut valleys of Grand Canyon National Park, in Arizona.

Pollution in the air gives this sunset in Los Angeles its orange colour.

The USA is a consumer society with a high standard of living. It uses huge amounts of energy and produces vast amounts of waste. As a largely urban society, it is dependent on the car for the majority of its transport. All of these factors have an effect on the natural environment.

Carbon emissions from homes and industries add to the percentage of carbon dioxide in the atmosphere, which leads to global warming. Other gases released into the atmosphere help create acid rain, and the acidification of rivers and lakes in areas such as the Appalachians and New Jersey.

Air pollution is a problem in most US cities, particularly in Los Angeles, where smog can be a daily event. Due to its location, Los Angeles often experiences a temperature inversion, where warm air overlies cold air. Harmful gases build up from car exhausts within this cold, stable layer. When they react with sunlight, they produce low-level ozone, a harmful irritant that can cause lung problems. When the temperature inversion is finally broken down by winds, the air pollution can travel inland and form a haze in the Grand Canyon, obscuring the view.

CASE STUDY
CHESAPEAKE BAY

Chesapeake Bay is the USA's largest estuary, situated on the east coast. The water in the Bay is a mixture of salt water from the Atlantic Ocean and fresh water from the rivers that drain into it. This leads to a variety of ecosystems, depending on the level of salinity at a particular location. Huge numbers of fish, shellfish and birds used to live in the bay. At one time, oysters could filter the entire waters of the bay in just a few days. Now it takes over a year.

Human settlement has caused changes in Chesapeake Bay. Over 15 million people now live in the catchment areas of the rivers that drain into it and along the coast. One problem is excessive nutrients, which find their way into the bay from agricultural run-offs and from sewage works. Both sources produce nitrates and phosphates, which encourage the growth of algae. These organisms block out light to the lower depths of water, and some plants cannot cope and die. When the algae die they sink to the bottom. As they decompose, oxygen is taken from the water. Some species of fish and other organisms cannot survive in the reduced oxygen levels, so they swim elsewhere or die.

A fisherman brings in his catch of blue crabs from the waters of Chesapeake Bay.

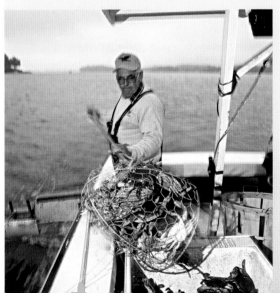

Water in the bay is less clear than it used to be. Cutting down upstream forests for agriculture has meant a great deal of sediment flows into the bay every year, and plants such as eel grass cannot survive well. If the grasses die, the water becomes even cloudier because the grasses help to trap sediment. They also slow down the movement of waves, so they protect the coastline from erosion. In the growing season, the grasses also absorb large amounts of nitrates and phosphates. Numbers of geese and other birds have gone down in the bay because they are dependent on the declining grasses for food.

Numbers of fish and shellfish are also falling because of over-harvesting. The removal of large numbers of shellfish means that the natural filtration system of the bay is being severely reduced.

In 1983, the Chesapeake Bay Agreement was drawn up. Its aim is to restore wildlife in the bay by dealing first with water quality. There has been a ban on the use of phosphate-based detergents throughout the area, and an education campaign has informed the public about their impact on the bay's ecosystem. Farmers are encouraged to minimise nitrate fertiliser use. The target of the agreement is to reduce excess nutrients by 40 per cent, and to continue to restore damaged habitats.

THE AMERICAN CITIZEN AND THE ENVIRONMENT

Although US citizens use more resources per head than any other nation, it does not mean that they are not concerned about their environment. The first national park was created in the USA and Americans are keen to conserve their landscapes for future generations. As people become more educated about environmental issues, they are more aware of their own impacts on the environment.

ENVIRONMENTAL ORGANISATIONS

There are many environmental organisations, both at a national and local level. One of the most well-known national organisations is the Sierra Club, which was founded in 1892. Today it has 700,000 members. The Club's aims include education to help protect and restore environments, and the responsible use of the earth's ecosystems and resources.

At a local level, many groups were set up as a result of the 1992 Rio Earth Summit's call to 'Think globally, act locally'. These groups work on local projects such as tree planting, organising local litter-collection days, or developing environmental awareness in their area.

ADOPT-A-HIGHWAY SCHEME

The Adopt-a-Highway programme operates across the whole of the USA. People, businesses or organisations take on responsibility for a stretch of highway for a period of one or two years. A sign is erected at the side of the road showing which group is looking after a particular stretch of highway, and the group keeps their stretch litter-free and tidy. In California there are more than 6,000 groups who keep more than 9,000km of roads clear of litter. Their combined labour has been worth $140 billion since the scheme began in the 1980s, and allows the authorities to concentrate their money on road repairs and improvements instead of litter collection.

RECYCLING

Recycling banks exist throughout the USA and are very common in California. In some areas residents are expected to sort their rubbish into glass, paper, plastic or organic wastes, which have separate banks. The lack of landfill space in which to put rubbish means the authorities want to recycle more and to encourage firms to use less packaging to reduce the waste going into landfill sites.

TRANSPORT

Americans are highly dependent on their cars, which creates a huge demand for oil and pollutes the atmosphere with emissions. In California the four-lane highways are often completely blocked during the rush hours. Along many sections there is now an extra lane, called the car pool lane, which can only be accessed by cars containing more than one person. This lane is less congested than the other lanes, so it encourages people to share their cars by allowing them to reach their destinations faster. The fewer cars on the road, the less damage to the environment. However, even in the rush hours, the car pool lane is often underused, showing that more needs to be done to encourage car sharing.

ACTION GROUPS

Numerous action groups campaign on a single issue in the USA. The Glen Canyon Action Network (GCAN) was set up to prevent further damage to the Colorado River and to try to reverse some of the damage already done. In 1963, a large dam was built on the Colorado and the Glen Canyon was flooded behind it, creating Lake Powell. The costs of the dam construction and maintenance have not yet been covered by the benefits of electricity production from the dam. The dam has also damaged the river's ecosystems and this, combined with its costs, has led the GCAN to campaign for the demolition of the dam, the draining of Lake Powell and the restoration of the spectacular Glen Canyon.

A row of recycling bins for bottles, or bottle banks, in California.

A SUSTAINABLE FUTURE?

To develop sustainably, a country must use its resources without affecting the needs of future generations. At present, within the USA, this is not the case. The growing population is using more energy and resources than ever before.

American cars are more efficient today, but there are more of them. In California alone there are 22 million cars, which leads to congestion on the roads and a drain on fuel reserves. The country emits more greenhouse gases per person than any other nation. These gases include carbon dioxide, methane and nitrous oxides, which are emitted from car exhausts, industries, power stations and domestic heating systems. The amount is linked to the high standard of living enjoyed by the average American, but there are not enough fuel reserves to sustain this level of use.

KYOTO

In 1998 the USA agreed to and signed the Kyoto Protocol, and agreed to reduce its greenhouse gas emissions by 5 per cent by the year 2010. In June 2001, soon after he was elected president, President George W. Bush withdrew the USA from this agreement because he felt it would damage the country's economy. This decision has separated the USA from the majority of other developed world nations, who are using the target set by Kyoto as the minimum they should try to achieve. The people of the USA have a mixed view. A poll conducted in March 2001 showed that citizens of the USA thought in a more sustainable way than their government, and were more in tune with the other developed nations of the world. When asked the best way to solve the country's energy crisis, 56 per cent responded that the solution should be by conservation, where people use less energy and therefore produce less carbon dioxide. California leads the way in reducing the amounts of energy used by each citizen, and with government help these ideas could be used by other states to reduce greenhouse gas emissions.

Demonstrators in June 2001 protest against President George W. Bush's decision to withdraw the USA from agreements to reduce its greenhouse gas emissions.

Police and firefighters begin the long and distressing job of clearing up after the attack on the World Trade Center.

Sometimes in its past the USA has been unwilling to become involved in international affairs. This changed forever on 11 September 2001, when the World Trade Center and the Pentagon were bombed by terrorists flying hijacked planes.

THE WORLD'S LOSS

In the space of a few minutes more than 3,000 people were killed in the suicide attacks. The exact number will never be known, as many bodies were impossible to identify. Although most of the dead were Americans, people of many other nationalities, including several hundred British citizens, were also killed. Almost the whole world was horrified by what had happened: one of the few people to praise the bombers was Osama bin Laden, who was soon identified as the likely leader of the terrorist plotters.

THE USA RESPONDS

Very quickly President George W. Bush began to organise an Alliance of the world's nations to fight the terrorist threat. One of his closest allies was the British prime minister, Tony Blair, who travelled around the world to persuade national leaders to join the Alliance. The Allies began a military campaign against Afghanistan and its ruling party, the Taliban, who were sheltering bin Laden and refusing to give him up for trial. By early 2002 the Alliance and its allies inside Afghanistan had pushed the Taliban from power, but by November 2004 they still had not captured bin Laden. No one was sure whether he had escaped or been killed in the bombing raids.

In March 2003 the USA widened its 'War on Terror' when, with troops from the UK and other countries, it invaded Iraq. The Iraqi leader, Saddam Hussein, was captured in December 2003. However, by December 2004, US and British soldiers were still suffering frequent attacks by Iraqis loyal to Saddam and by terrorists intent on driving out the Allies.

Acid rain Moisture reaching the ground that contains sulphuric and nitric acids, produced by burning fossil fuels and absorbed by the clouds from the air.

Barrier island A low, sandy bank that develops off gently sloping coasts.

Biomass power Energy produced from plant material or vegetation.

Branding A name or mark used by a company to distinguish its goods from those of other companies.

Coniferous Trees that bear cones and are usually evergreen.

Consumer society A society that buys goods, such as clothes and food.

Convection currents Currents caused by the expansion of a gas or a liquid when its temperature rises. In the semi-solid rock of the earth's mantle, convection currents cause the plates to move.

Cumulonimbus clouds Very large, thick clouds that grow vertically and tower to a great height. They look dark at the base because they are so thick.

Deciduous Broadleaved trees, such as oaks, that drop their leaves in autumn.

Delta A triangular-shaped area of land near the mouths of some rivers where sediment is deposited by rivers as they meet the sea.

Deposition The act of depositing.

Distributaries The branches of rivers that flow away from the main stream.

Drainage basin The area that is drained by a river and its tributaries.

Ecosystems Communities of animals and plants, and the environments in which they live.

Emissions Waste gases and solids discharged into the atmosphere from factory chimneys and vehicle exhausts.

Emission laws Maximum levels of emissions set by governments to control air pollution.

Epicentre The point on the surface of the earth directly above the focus of an earthquake.

Estuary The mouth of a river where fresh water meets salt water.

Fossil fuels Fuels that have formed over millions of years and have been preserved, or fossilised. The main fossil fuels are coal, oil and gas.

Global warming The gradual warming of the surface of the planet as a result of a change in the composition of atmospheric gases, especially an increase in the percentage of carbon dioxide.

Greenhouse gases Gases that help to trap warmth in the atmosphere, which contributes to global warming.

Gross Domestic Product (GDP) The total value of goods produced by a country's economy.

Gross National Income (GNI) The total value of everything produced by industry and services within a country and earned by that country abroad.

Hi-tech industries High technology industries. These are industries that use the latest production techniques and technology, such as aerospace, computing and electronics.

Hurricane Violent tropical storm that forms over warm seas. The high-speed winds spiral round a central calm area called the eye.

Industrial base The main types of work providing income for an economy.

Levee A bank at the side of a river that has been naturally formed when the river has overflowed and dropped sediment.

Mechanisation The process of using machines to do work previously done by people or animals.

Microchips Miniature and complex electronic circuits.

Migrant A person who moves away from his or her home. The move can be temporary, like a holiday, or permanent.

Permafrost A layer of permanently frozen soil, found near the surface of the arctic regions.

Plain A large area of flat land.

Plate One of several sections of the earth's crust composed of rock several kilometres thick, which can be thousands of kilometres wide.

Plateau A raised area of relatively flat land.

Prairie A large area of land with grass and few or no trees.

Private investment Money from individuals rather than companies.

Rain shadow An area on the leeward side of a mountain range that receives relatively little rainfall because most has already fallen on the windward side.

Recession A period of temporary business shortage, when unemployment and poverty levels rise.

Richter scale A scale used to measure the magnitude (size) of an earthquake.

Scrub Vegetation consisting of stunted trees or shrubs.

Spit A ridge of sand or shingle that projects out into the sea. It is joined to the land at one end.

Spur A ridge or hill that projects from the main mass of land.

Stacks Tall pillars of rock, detached from the main part of a cliff and rising out of the sea.

Tax incentives A method used by governments to encourage businesses and people to produce or buy something by reducing the tax they have to pay on it.

Tornado A violent revolving storm formed over rapidly heated land.

Trading deficit The amount by which a sum of money falls short.

Tributary A river that joins a larger river.

Tundra A high latitude region where it is too cold for trees to grow. The vegetation consists of lichens, mosses and grasses.

FURTHER INFORMATION

BOOKS TO READ:

Country Fact Files: The USA by John Baines (Hodder Wayland, 1998) Illustrated reference for KS2–3.

Country Studies: USA by Olly Phillipson (Heinemann Library, 1998) Illustrated reference for KS2–3.

History of the USA (Hodder & Stoughton Educational, 2000) Overview of the entire history of the USA.

Modern America by Jon Nichol & Chris MacDonald (Nelson Thornes, 1996) Textbook for GCSE covering the USA since 1914.

Modern World Revision: Pack 4 by Philip Stanton (Nelson Thornes, 1999) A pack for GCSE covering the USA from 1919–1941.

The Native Peoples of North America by Martin Whittock (Hodder & Stoughton Educational, 2001) Textbook for KS3 covering the history and cultural diversity of indigenous North American peoples.

North America: An Advanced Geography by Brian Price & Paul Guiness (Hodder & Stoughton Educational, 1997) Textbook for 16–19 year-olds covering both the USA and Canada.

The Rough Guide to the USA by Samantha Cook, Tim Perry & Greg Ward (Rough Guides, 2000) A comprehensive handbook to the USA, with practical tips and state-by-state commentary.

WEBSITES:

CITIES
Boston's new expressway: www.mrtunnel.com

Las Vegas Review Journal: www.lvrj.com

RIVERS
www.americanrivers.org

TRANSPORT
www.bts.gov/

www.bts.gov/transtu/

INDUSTRY AND WORK
http://stats.bls.gov/data

PEOPLE
Census data: www.census.gov/index.html

The Navajo nation:
www.americanwest.com/pages/navajo2.htm

GENERAL INFORMATION ON THE USA
News updates: www.cnn.com

General information on all states:
www.globalcomputing.com/states.html

Energy and the Environment: www.eia.doe.gov/

Nuclear waste issue in Nevada:
www.state.nv.us/nucwaste/

Grand Canyon: www.nps.gov/grca/index.htm

Everglades: www.nps.gov/ever/home.htm

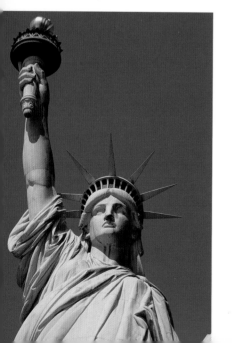

The Statue of Liberty, New York City.

Manhattan, New York City, at sunset.